NEOVENATOR

and Other Dinosaurs of Europe

by Dougal Dixon

illustrated by
Steve Weston and **James Field**

PICTURE WINDOW BOOKS
Minneapolis, Minnesota

Picture Window Books
5115 Excelsior Boulevard
Suite 232
Minneapolis, MN 55416
877-845-8392
www.picturewindowbooks.com

Printed in the United States of America.

Library of Congress Cataloging-in-Publication Data
Dixon, Dougal.
Neovenator and other dinosaurs of Europe / by
Dougal Dixon ; illustrated by Steve Weston & James
Field.
p. cm. — (Dinosaur find)
Includes bibliographical references and index.
ISBN-13: 978-1-4048-2264-1 (library binding)
ISBN-10: 1-4048-2264-X (library binding)
ISBN-13: 978-1-4048-2270-2 (paperback)
ISBN-10: 1-4048-2270-4 (paperback)
1. Dinosaurs–Europe–Juvenile literature. I. Weston,
Steve, ill. II. Field, James, 1959- ill. III. Title.
QE861.5.D625 2007
567.9094–dc22   2006028005

Acknowledgments
This book was produced for Picture Window Books by
Bender Richardson White, U.K.

Illustrations by James Field (cover and pages 1, 4–5,
7, 9, 11, 17) and Steve Weston (pages 13, 15, 19, 21).
Diagrams by Stefan Chabluk.

Photographs: Corbis Inc page 8. Getty Images pages
10, 20. istockphotos pages 6 (Goran Mottram), 12
(Paul Wolf), 14, 16 (Vladimir Pomortsev), 18 (Steffen
Foerster).

Consultant: John Stidworthy, Scientific Fellow of
the Zoological Society, London, and former
Lecturer in the Education Department, Natural History
Museum, London.

Reading Adviser: Susan Kesselring, M.A., Literacy
Educator, Rosemount–Apple Valley–Eagan
(Minnesota) School District

Types of dinosaurs
In this book, a red shape at the
top of a left-hand page shows
the animal was a meat-eater.
A green shape shows it was
a plant-eater.

Just how big—or small— were they?
Dinosaurs were many different
sizes. We have compared their
size to one of the following:

Chicken
2 feet (60 centimeters) tall
Weight 6 pounds (2.7 kilograms)

Adult person
6 feet (1.8 meters) tall
Weight 170 pounds (76.5 kg)

Elephant
10 feet (3 m) tall
Weight 12,000 pounds
(5,400 kg)

TABLE OF CONTENTS

WHAT'S INSIDE?

Dinosaurs! These dinosaurs lived in the places that now form Europe. Find out how they survived millions of years ago and what they have in common with today's animals.

Life in Europe

Dinosaurs lived between 230 million and 65 million years ago. The world did not look the same then. Much of the land and many of the seas were not in the same places as today.. The land of what became Europe was mostly swamps and lakes, surrounded by low hills and high mountains. Dinosaurs lived in all these areas.

On the edge of a lake, two *Eotyrannus* were ready to feed on the body of a dead *Iguanodon*. But a much bigger meat-eater, *Neovenator,* was about to chase them away. It would then eat the *Iguanodon* remains.

IGUANODON

Pronunciation:
ih-GWAN-o-dahn

Iguanodon was a large plant-eater. It used its beak to pull and tear off leaves and twigs for food. Then *Iguanodon* used teeth at the back of its mouth to crush the food. This dinosaur sometimes walked on all fours and sometimes on its hind legs.

Dangerous feeding sites today

Modern sheep often feed on grass close to the edge of cliffs. Sometimes, one loses its footing and falls over the cliff, as *Iguanodon* once did.

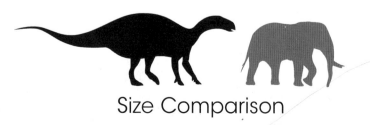

Size Comparison

An *Iguanodon* tried to reach plants growing near the top of a cliff but tumbled over the edge. Many years later, its remains would be discovered as fossils.

7

NEOVENATOR

Pronunciation:
KNEE-o-vuh-NAT-tur

Neovenator was a big meat-eater that prowled the swamps, hunting for plant-eating dinosaurs. It killed with long teeth and sharp claws. After eating a large animal, the *Neovenator* might not have had another meal for several weeks. It rested between hunting trips.

Resting after meals today

Modern hyenas are scavengers and will rest for a long time after a big meal, as *Neovenator* did.

Size Comparison

Neovenator was always on the lookout for food. It was a scavenger. It scared off flying reptiles called *Pterosaurs* that were also looking for dead animals to eat.

EOTYRANNUS

Pronunciation:
EE-o-tye-RAN-us

Eotyrannus was one of the smaller meat-eaters of what is now Europe. It was an early relative of the famous *Tyrannosaurus* but not nearly as large. Like most small meat-eaters, *Eotyrannus* was covered in feathers. It hunted even smaller animals in the swampy forests.

Feathered hunter today

The modern bateleur eagle is a small, fierce, feathered scavenger, like *Eotyrannus* was long ago.

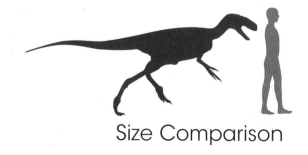

Size Comparison

Eotyrannus prowled among ferns and bushes, looking for a small animal to chase or a dead body to feed on.

SCELIDOSAURUS

Pronunciation:
skel-EYE-doe-SAW-rus

Scelidosaurus was one of the first armored dinosaurs. Its head, neck, back, and tail were covered with studs and plates. The armor protected *Scelidosaurus* against attacks by meat-eating dinosaurs.

Keeping dry today

Modern water birds, like this night heron, are quite happy in the rain. Water just runs off their feathers, like rain ran off the armor of *Scelidosaurus*.

Size Comparison

The armor of *Scelidosaurus* was so thick and tough that heavy rain likely rolled right off the dinosaur's back.

STRUTHIOSAURUS

Pronunciation:
STROO-thee-o-SAW-rus

Imagine an armored dinosaur, all horns and spikes. Now imagine it smaller than a sheep! That is what *Struthiosaurus* looked like. It lived on islands where there was not much food. Today, there are other types of small animals living on such islands.

Small animals today

The Shetland pony is a small mammal. Like *Struthiosaurus*, the pony is an island animal. It comes from the Shetland Isles of Scotland.

Size Comparison

14

Little *Struthiosaurus* fed on plants growing on the ground. It ignored the tiny lizard-like animals that ran among the plants.

CETIOSAURISCUS

Pronunciation:
SEE-tee-uh-SAW-ris-kus

Cetiosauriscus was a long-necked plant-eater. Its neck was especially long. This dinosaur also had a very long and powerful tail. It used that tail as a weapon. *Cetiosauriscus* swung its tail at hungry meat-eaters that tried to attack.

Tail weapon today

A monitor lizard uses its tail to beat off attackers, just as *Cetiosauriscus* did.

Size Comparison

Cetiosauriscus used its long tail like a whip to keep off a *Neovenator*, a big meat-eater.

EFRAASIA

Efraasia was a plant-eater. The long-necked dinosaur sometimes walked on all fours, and sometimes on just its hind legs. It lived in hot areas, feeding on plants beside rivers and streams. To eat, *Efraasia* used its front teeth to scrape tough leaves from twigs.

Riverside today

Modern elephants gather at rivers in hot areas, just like *Efraasia* did.

Size Comparison

Efraasia ate near rivers and streams. Sometimes an *Efraasia* got caught in a fast-moving stream and died.

19

VARIRAPTOR

Pronunciation:
VA-ree-RAP-tor

Variraptor was a fierce little hunter. It had a killing claw on each hind foot and sharp, curved claws on its grasping hands. *Variraptor* was covered in feathers and probably looked like its more famous cousin, the *Velociraptor*.

Small hunter today

The modern kingfisher looks gentle but is a fierce hunter of fish. *Variraptor* also was tougher than it looked.

Size Comparison

Variraptor must have looked like a colorful bird as it hunted through the forests.

21

Where Did They Go?

Dinosaurs are extinct, which means that none of them are alive today. Scientists study rocks and fossils to find clues about what happened to dinosaurs.

People have different explanations about what happened. Some people think a huge asteroid hit Earth and caused all sorts of climate changes, which caused the dinosaurs to die. Others think volcanic eruptions caused the climate to change and that killed the dinosaurs. No one knows for sure what happened to all of the dinosaurs.

Glossary

armor—protective covering of plates, horns, spikes, or clubs used for fighting

beak—the hard front part of the mouth of birds and some dinosaurs; also called a bill

claws—tough, usually curved fingernails or toenails

ferns—plants with finely divided leaves known as fronds; ferns are common in damp woods and along rivers

fossils—the remains of a plant or animal that lived between thousands and millions of years ago

mammal—a warm-blooded animal that has hair and drinks mother's milk when it is young

plate—a large, flat structure on the body

prey—animals that are hunted by other animals for food; the hunters are known as predators

scavenger—a meat-eater that feeds on animals that are already dead

To Learn More

At the Library

Clark, Neil, and William Lindsay. *1001 Facts About Dinosaurs.* New York: Backpack Books, Dorling Kindersley, 2002.

Dixon, Dougal. *Dougal Dixon's Amazing Dinosaurs.* Honesdale, Pa.: Boyds Mills Press, 2000.

Holtz, Thomas, and Michael Brett-Surman. *Dinosaur Field Guide.* New York: Random House, 2001.

On the Web

FactHound offers a safe, fun way to find Web sites related to this book. All of the sites on FactHound have been researched by our staff.

1. Visit *www.facthound.com*
2. Type in this special code: 140482264X
3. Click on the FETCH IT button.

Your trusty FactHound will fetch the best Web sites for you!

Index

Look for all of the books in the Dinosaur Find series: